Harrison Moore

FLIPPING HOUSES

A Complete Guide to Learn How to Find, Buy and Rehab Houses to Rent or Resell, for Create Your Real Estate Investing Business

Copyright © 2020 publishing.

All rights reserved.

Author: Harrison Moore

No part of this publication may be reproduced, distributed or transmitted in any form or by any means, including photocopying recording or other electronic or mechanical methods or by any information storage and retrieval system without the prior written permission of the publisher, except in the case of brief quotation embodies in critical reviews and certain other non-commercial uses permitted by copyright law.

Table of Contents

The Art of Flipping Houses 6

Things You Need to Know About Flipping Houses 15

Benefits of Flipping Houses 18

Flipping Houses - A How To Guide 23

The Beginner's Guide to Flipping Houses 27

Flipping Houses - Is it the Job For You? 31

Flipping Houses Ethics 34

Is Flipping Houses Legal? 55

Does Flipping Houses Break the Law? 61

The Philosophy of Flipping Houses 65

How to Start Flipping Houses 68

The Best Cities For Flipping Houses 70

Basic Steps to Flipping Houses For Profit 74

Succeeding in Flipping Houses 79

Fixing and Flipping Houses For Profit - How Much to Renovate?. 83

Flipping Houses and Lease Purchase Agreement 86

The Rules of Flipping Houses 90

Wholesaling Real Estate Vs Rehabbing and Flipping Houses 92

Working in Real Estate - Jobs Like Flipping Houses 98

Rehabbing Ugly Houses Will Give You Beautiful Profits 104

Flip Houses Online 112

Understanding Confusing Contracts 119

Tax Reporting for Flipping Houses 122

Tempted By Low Mortgage Rates? Why Not To Stop Flipping Houses 124

The Perfect Way to Make Profit in the Current Economic Down Turn 127

Avoiding Dealer Status When Flipping Houses 129

Flipping Homes With Wholesale Loans 132

The Art of Flipping Houses

To really understand the turn houses upside down, you could compare it to something else. Have you ever considered the metaphor of art?

Metaphors are one of the best ways to understand anything. If you really want to learn something new, speed up the process, deepen learning... embrace and compare the new subject with something you already know. Something you know. Something simple.

It's a metaphor. It's comparative learning. The greatest teachers of world history have used metaphors over and over again to anchor their teachings in others. The method works because it applies a fundamental truth about human understanding. That is the concept of being relative.

We understand the things, concepts and realities of WHAT ARE NOT.

We know it's high... because we understand low. We've known for a long time... because we understand short. We know it's hot... because we understand the cold.

And vice versa.

And so, flipping houses is also compared to other things. In this debate, art.

And what is art? Well, we must consider the definition of art: beauty, expression, individuality. Creativity and passion. There are many ways to understand art, to understand what it really means. And one way to understand art is to "take something bad, or basic, and make it something beautiful, or refined."

Looks like they're going to send me houses. On the one hand, returning a house means having a house that could use a facelift. Maybe even a major operation. Laid, of course, he needs repairs. Often, the more damaged and dilapidated it is, the better.

These kind of houses make stellar fins. You have to start with little to do much.

For another, flipping a house means having the ability to upgrade, tear, lift, break and tie. Creation and design. A home flip project needs teams to do the job, and do it properly. Anyone who has worked in this area understands the importance of the crew. There are too many problems for any home renovation project to work with unequal or unskilled workers.

The project of overturning the house is similar to a painting canvas that a painter needs. The paintings alone will not inspire anyone. But give an experienced and artistic painter some brushes and paint... and white canvases, and soon there will be something to look at and talk about. Something precious.

Finally, upside houses can be compared to art because presentation counts in art. A beautiful painting needs a beautiful frame. A finely designed figurine needs an elegant base. A book of greed needs a provocative cover. Despite this, a renovated home for sale needs some finishing touches, accents such as stage furniture, washed windows and mowed lawns. The house also needs a marketing plan: expressive photos and eye-catching descriptions.

The case of reversal is better understood by comparing it with concepts that are similar, but are of a different subject. Art is a different subject, yes, but incredibly similar, because the process of change and creation in art is very similar to the process we go through when we topple the houses.

Most people who return from homes for a living do not consider themselves artists. But I can assure you... Are.

Flipping Still Works in Today's Market?

These days (in this weak housing market), when I tell non-investors that I return homes to live, I usually get a surprised or skeptical look in return. Beginning comment most of them is, "I think things are pretty tough for you these days."

Fortunately for me (and for you!), this is as far from the truth as possible. Here's what non-investors don't understand:

In real estate, there is never a good time to be both buying and selling real estate. In a typical high-end market, homes are easy to sell (there are many motivated buyers), but it is difficult to find much when buying. In a typical low market, homes are easy to buy (there are many motivated sellers), but it's hard to turn around to find a lot of demand to resell your properties. In a secondary market (where prices don't change much), it can be a bit difficult to buy and sell homes.

If the turnaround required both a large market to buy and a large market to sell at the same time, there would never have been a good time to return homes. Fortunately, it is not so.

For a large flip market, you need to be able to buy real estate at a huge discount or you need to be able to sell real estate at a good premium – you don't need both. In much of the country, today's market still meets the criteria to be able to buy at a big discount, and in some large markets we are beginning to see a recovery that allows investors to sell back at a premium.

Of course, selling is harder now than it was (perhaps harder than in 30 years), but it is certainly not impossible. The key to finding the sellers that are there, is to buy good properties at the right price, both are very easy to do in today's market. In fact, I'm going to spend a lot of this book focusing on exactly how to buy the right property at the right price, so stay with me, and you'll soon see why enter the market of today is not so difficult.

How Much Can I Earn By Throwing Houses?

Not surprisingly, the biggest question on the minds of potential investors is: "how much money can I make by launching houses?"

First, there is no correct answer to this question. Of course, part-time fins will be hard to earn as much as full-time fins. Also, someone living in California may be able to make $100.000 on a typical flip compared to someone in the Nebraska rural that may be able to average $10,000 on each of their flips (regardless of differences in cost and risk as well).

However, since this is a major issue, let me give you an idea of what a typical corporate turnaround might look like. In fact, let's take my business as an example, because I live in a fairly typical real estate market, and we focus on the types of homes many fins target the Home.

Before starting hiring employees, I found it not very difficult to handle on average one or two jumps a month, alone, with the help of a realtor to find and resell properties. On average, I earn about $ 20,000 in profit on each flip. Therefore, in a year, I could average $ 240,000 to $ 480,000 in profit, with no employees to manage!

Now I have two full-time employees in my company-different from me. One is my wife, who has her own real estate license, and is responsible for all marketing and real estate agent activities. The other is a full-time project manager who is responsible for researching, hiring and managing contractors and ensuring that projects are on schedule and on budget.

In between, they manage about 90% of the daily work required by the company, while I manage the remaining 10% and focus on our future strategy and growth. With the three of us, the company could potentially handle about 3-5 Flip per month, creating a gross annual profit of over $ 1,000,000! (Although the three of us also focus on many other commercial interests, so we're actually still averaging about 1-2 launches per month).

Even a part-time pinball player who has a full-time job can easily switch from two to four houses a year. With an average profit of $ 20,000-25,000 per flip, there are no excuses why an average person shouldn't be able to make an extra $50,000 to $100,000 per year by launching homes in his spare time.

What About Taxes?

As long as I have delighted you with all the money you can earn by throwing houses, this is probably the right time to remember the bad news: you will pay taxes on your profits. Your" profits " are what remains from the sale of the house, after deducting the cost of rehabilitation (labor and materials), fixed costs (fees, commissions, closing costs loan, taxes, insurance, utilities, etc), and any other costs directly related to the purchase, repair, and/or the sale of the home.

You may have heard that investment income is taxed more favorably than other corporate income, but unfortunately, the money earned by returning homes is not considered investment income. As a domestic pinball machine, you buy and sell a commodity - it's no different if you buy and sell shoes, furniture, cars or food. As such, you will probably pay the same percentage of taxes as you would if that income came from any other type of activity or even from full-time employment. In addition to income tax, you will probably have to pay another 13-15% of taxes on self-employment, at least on a part of the income.

I will not lie-taxes will eat significantly in your profits. But, in my opinion, it is better to earn a lot and pay taxes than not to earn a lot in the first place. I highly recommend that once you take the decision that you are serious about to be in the house flipping business (either part-time or full-time), that you consult a qualified accountant or CPA who can help you structure your business in a way that will allow you to pay the lowest possible amount of taxes.

Things You Need to Know About Flipping Houses

Flipping houses provides a great opportunity to earn money in a single project. Home flipping is the art of buying a home and securing it for rental or resale. I call it art because there is no specific rule to follow to get a positive return on investment. It is an investment opportunity that involves creativity, careful planning, budgeting and know - how in order to reap the golden fruits of a property.

You might think it's a cliché, but location is very important to identify a symmetry property. I would rather buy a house that is consumed in a marketable neighborhood, than go with a very nice house in a less popular place. Once the house is repaired, it is important to sell it as soon as possible so that the project is profitable. Houses located in the main neighborhoods attract quality buyers who can pay you in full or give a large down payment for the House.

Obsolete homes and mobile homes are great prospects as these properties can be purchased at very low prices. These so-called" Rod Fixer" is perfect for home flipping as they offer you a fantastic opportunity to turn some naughty duck into a swan. Not only do you get fixer on at much lower prices, but there is also less competition in buying these homes. Fixators on them are usually sold to many that works for the benefit of an investor.

It is very important to create a detailed plan of your financial goal. Determine the parts of the house that need to be repaired and calculate the costs that you need to do. Also try to define a profit margin that you ideally want. Include this percentage in your budget to make sure you get very positive feedback from your home flipping project.

Since flipping homes involves a lot of renovation and fixing, you need to remember that buyers are more attracted to beautiful homes than they can show their friends. A beautiful exterior would be a beautiful landscape, painted fences, beautiful windows and screens and new lighting fixtures, among other things. A beautiful interior would be recently installed carpets, wallpapers and suspended ceilings. These things are relatively inexpensive, but they add a lot of value to the House.

If you are going to stay in the company for a long time to launch the house, buying bulk materials would be a great idea. This saves money rather than buying fewer items that can be expensive. I like to set a color theme for some of my home flipping projects. This way I buy the items at much cheaper prices and do not run out of materials once the renovations begin.

Marketing the property while the work is in progress continues to work for me. Invite buyers to come and take a look at the house even while the renovations are underway. Keep buyers in the light of things and send a picture of how the House will look once improvements are made.

In the Beautiful Houses, time is of great essence. Renovation work should be carried out quickly, and the House should be sold once the project is completed. Finding the right property to return also plays an important role as well as budgeting to maximize profits. With all these things in mind, launching a house is a beautiful project that offers many opportunities to earn large sums of money. It is a great source of income that has provided financial security for many people.

Benefits of Flipping Houses

The most obvious advantage of returning homes is, of course, the potentially significant capital gain that can be made.

There are however some other more abstract perks that you need to be aware of embarking on stunning homes to realize your real estate wealth.

As with most things in life there are many pros and cons associated with returning homes.

Many things can be learned by browsing the homes, the experience and knowledge you will gain can certainly be used in many other situations in life.

Budget - There aren't many things that can teach you how to budget with the speed with which you launch your homes.

While launching a house, you need to know/learn to budget quickly or lose a lot of money.

Two skills that are very important regarding home flips is to set a budget and stick to it.

Once you've learned this ability, you'll be surprised at how many opportunities will appear in other aspects of life.

Muscle definition - You see, flipping home can be very good exercise.

This is very true for people who do most of the work themselves (this is recommended when you want to cut these expensive, labor consumption costs).

Attention to detail - Every time you return a home this capacity will be improved. With houses spinning, small things can make a big difference. The key is not to overlook the little things like proper staging, electric apse plates, and a good eye for color throughout the property. It is very important that the buyer sees the property as a place that has been cared for rather than seeing it as just another place on their list that they need to see today. This is an advantage that can be used in all areas of life. You'll start looking at everything differently, from your relationships to tax preparation.

Positive thinking - You have probably heard many times, many people the importance of positive thinking is. This is very true with the turnaround of the house.

It's always good to add a little reality to your positive thinking from time to time, but you have to be aware that positive thinking is very powerful in flipping houses and most other aspects of life.

Someone once said, "Everything in life is easy when you're positive, the hardest part is being positive every day."

Just Do It - Ahh, the old Nike slogan. If the reversal of the houses teaches you one thing, it would be that. Every day you own the house, you carry your expenses (mortgage, interest, etc.). Everything becomes easier after the start. Rather than worrying about all the things that might go wrong, just do it and don't think too much.

It is always useful to be able to estimate the intrinsic value of the property. This comes with a combination of experience and market research. Take a walk around your neighborhood and take a look at all the "for sale" signs. Take a diary and start seeing what the houses are going for. Once you have a sense of how much a house is worth, you will be surprised how many good opportunities begin to look at their heads. And as you improve this ability, more possibilities appear.

Launch houses are not rocket science, but it takes a unique combination of luck, skill and stubbornness to make a profit in this particular business. Learning the lessons above will not only help you succeed when it comes to returning homes, but also in other aspects of your life.

Although flipping houses isn't the hardest thing in the world, it takes a unique combination of skill, luck, research and stubbornness to make a profit. By learning the above skills, you are guaranteed success in turning houses upside down and in life. You will find that all the time, effort and labor are actually small prices to pay for the knowledge and experience you will get.

Flipping Houses - A How To Guide

Flipping homes is an amazing way to make huge profits in a relatively short period of time. I am sure you've seen the shows, "Flip This House," or "Flip That House" or even "Property Scale." These show all the fins of new houses that buy houses in distress, repair them, then sell them and make crazy profits. These shows tend to show that the most dramatic parts of the company's turnaround at home and I can understand that. After all, it's television. Maybe some of the other details, like finding these offers, how to determine what constitutes a deal and what costs they don't tell us, are not very exciting, but these are the things you need to know before you get into the real estate investment game. In this article, I'll fill in the gaps and show you the things you should know if you really want to learn how to flip the houses.

How to find cheap homes that are perfect to come back

There are a myriad of ways to find homes that would make the perfect flip. The important thing to understand is that you must buy a house with a very deep discount. Think about who would need to sell their home and would be willing to sell at that discount. The motivation of the seller is what we are really interested in. Sellers who are motivated to sell are those who face foreclosure, behind property tax payments, going through divorce, inheriting a property, people who need a house that needs too much repair, someone who buys another house and can't afford two houses, a landlord who is sick of tenants, and the list goes on and on.

Many reasons for this are found in the local courthouse of the county. You know the court and where to find that information. Many counties now have their data online. Look for public documents and find people who have the motivation to sell their property. Send them a letter telling them that you are a local investor and are interested in buying their As-Is property.

You can also drive neighborhoods and look for empty houses. These are usually easy to spot as the yard is usually overrun, there may be a broken window, there could be a lot of rubbish on the porch, there could be an old post that has piled up, etc. send them a letter saying you would buy their house for free.

What constitutes a Great House Flip Deal

Once you have found a motivated seller who wants to sell their property, you need to determine if it is a good deal for a flip. You'll need to know what the house will sell for. Get in touch with a local and informal real estate agent that you will buy and sell houses and want to build a relationship with them. Ask him if he would care if he would run comparable to the property. They will be able to tell you what they think they should sell for fixed.

Most real estate investors want to buy homes at 70% of the resale value, minus repair costs. So take 70% of the amount you have been quoted by the realtor and subtract the costs to get the house in saleable conditions. This will be your maximum authorized offer. Don't offer more than that. You can determine repair costs by taking different contractors from the house and having them give offers. Most entrepreneurs will do it for free.

70% of the resale value covers the costs you will probably have to pay when you own and sell the house. These are usually things like interest payments on any loan, utilities, insurance payments, real estate agent fees when you sell, closing service costs when you sell, property taxes and your profit. The last one is very important.

The Beginner's Guide to Flipping Houses

Flipping houses is a great way to make money in real estate. Buy a property, solve the problem, and then sell it for profit. These three things are the basic principles of domestic overturning, where the investor can earn significant profits. An Investor who can buy, repair and then sell a house rapidly emerges with money and profits that he can use to fund his next real estate investment.

Buying property

This is the first thing you must do to start throwing houses away. However, consider the financing that you will need to buy real estate. Do you have money to buy land? Will you apply for a bank loan? Do you have a partner with whom you can share the cost of buying a house? Depending on your financial situation, funding and financing are important things that you need to consider before buying a home to return.

When buying a house, the location and construction quality of the property is considered. Choose a house in a very good neighborhood so that the property is easy to sell later. It also determines the necessary improvements. Check for leaks and damaged floors, pipes, and roofs. Try to assess whether the house you are considering is worth it. Usually experienced home flippers choose Properties where they are required minor repairs, such as installing new carpet, painting, and gardening.

Your goal is to make money, while it would be nice to buy a property that is worth less than the market value. Finding a motivated seller is one way to buy a house at a low price. These motivated sellers are people who want to sell their homes for quick money. Transferring work, divorce or death in the family can force people to sell their house at very low prices.

Affected properties are also cheap homes that you can view. Search for extracts from records in the log, and see if you can apply for property. However, be very careful as some foreclosed properties don't offer an overview of the house, and so that no idea of its commercialization.

Buying a home for a return involves several factors, and this is the location, price and structural value. Start by buying real estate for the average American family. Usually it is a house with 3 bedrooms, two bathrooms, living room, kitchen, dining room, garage and beautiful garden.

Repair of the House

Renovations and upgrades are other things you should do in turning home. Set the budget for materials, work and overheads that you need to do. Find out if you want to hire a contractor to work, or make a repair yourself. Try to find the cheapest job, if possible. You, the older son and the students who need the money, you can fix everything.

In addition to drawing up a budget, you must also have a timetable for the project. Time is the essence of the house to throw as a house that is too long on the market is no longer profitable. Usually the House must be sold within 90 days of purchase.

When repairing a house, focus on those aspects that can increase the value of the property. One of them is a groomed lawn, as well as replacing broken electrical wires and plumbing. Make a detailed description of the materials and objects that you will need for the whole project. Keep the House simple and clean but attractive design.

Sell The House.

It all depends on eventually selling the house for profit by throwing houses. Organize an open day and invite people to come and see the house you are selling. Put the event on the market and inform as many people about it as possible.

You can prepare and send leaflets to your friends. Write a press release about the house and talk about property on social networks and forums. Use descriptive words and phrases when talking about property to people. Instead of saying "House for sale," write "modern opulence or" Twilight cottage." Try to sell the property as quickly as possible.

Returning home orders an average income of at least $ 25,000, which is not bad for investing in real estate. Maybe that's not what you have to do to make more money. Invest in home turnover projects and enter a world where huge profits can be generated in a short time.

Flipping Houses - Is it the Job For You?

First, we need to look at our finances to see if we can afford to take a second home and renovate it. You should have an idea of how much your total budget is going to be for the project, and be sure to factor in other costs that you need to add value on this project at home, if you are going to get a good return. In particular, entrepreneurs take more time than expected to complete the project, because things are likely to take more time than previously thought, and therefore extra money even for small and unexpected extras.

Once you have a fixed budget, the first step is to find a home that you think is worth returning. You need to be able to add value to this home while maintaining tight control over your finances in order to make a good profit. With your property already in mind, looking for a house worth renovating that is within your budget and at the same time that will be easy to sell can be very difficult to find. There are many people out there trying to get home, so finding one for yourself can be a real chore.

Once you have decided on your property, you need to go through the entire buying process. You can expect delays and make sure you have the property evaluated by an independent appraiser. Also, be aware that purchase costs may vary in order to obtain an early estimate of purchase costs.

So, the house is yours. And now? The best thing to do is to evaluate what needs to be done. From electricity to plumbing to interior design, returning a home right is a huge undertaking, and you need to be willing to spend and borrow money. In to add enough value to the property to get a good return on your investment.

Once the renovations have begun, be prepared to devote a lot of time, if necessary, to the project. Things that you can actually do yourself, will save you a lot of money, but do not be afraid to call an expert for a more important job.

Once the property looks the way you planned, have it revalued, and once you're ready to sell, don't be afraid to try non-traditional methods of selling, such as the Internet or out-of-town newspapers. You need so many eyes on your upside down home so that you can sell it as quickly as possible and stop having to make payments on it. The longer your property, the less successful your home will be.

Home flipping has become a fashionable way to earn money for many people. But be prepared to enter into this investment of your eyes and your pocket, wide open.

Flipping Houses Ethics

"Reputation is better than great wealth..."Proverbs 22: 1

Since I started my career launching houses in 1998, I saw a disturbing trend develop and continue to pick up speed, when it comes to ethics in real estate investing.

In my opinion, the management of your real estate investment business is an impeccable element. In their homes I wrote the whole chapter by that I'm not supposed to read other educational materials that my students know exactly what I think about it. But I think it's time to write a series of articles on this topic and address some of the ethical issues I see my fellow real estate investors give up.

And the first problem I would like to address is the value of your word.

I have a common scenario:

Answer Joe.

"Joe" is a real estate investor at wholesale-this means that his mission is to find homes at wholesale (in market), get them under a purchase contract, and then assign his interest as buyer to another real estate investor who will close in his place. Joe will charge a fee in exchange for selling his equitable interest in the contract, and the investor closes the purchase will have a lot to maintain or repair and return.

Joe throws houses at the wholesale market, which is not immoral. Similarly, most industries work-wholesale and retail. And Joe's not selling the house, he's selling his interest in the contract, but this is a discussion for another time.

So investor Joe finds a motivated seller with a property that you think could be a good deal..ma not sure. Then he makes an offer. Sales counter offers. Bingo, Joe might have something here.

As I wrote in previous articles, this is the point where Joe should stop and really do your due diligence on this property. Goes above and beyond the mere smell of the deal, Joe should stop and really analyze the numbers, the market and even its potential investor-buyers to see if they feel confident about it before moving on to finish things with the seller.

But it's a bit too much work for investor Joe right now-and that's where things are starting to fall apart.

Joe decided to go ahead and say, "Hey, no problem. If this case turns out to stink, I'll use my clause to pull back-no damage, no foul."

Isn't that bad, Joe? Really?

Immoral Safety Net

You see, Joe has a line in the contract that says: "this contract is subject to approval from the partner of the buyer."

Who's Joe's partner? That must be her cat, Fluffy. Or maybe his wife, who is not so excited about Joe's mental hospital, which still works and probably would have questioned all of Joe's contract, if you leave her.

That's really happening. Joe understands that later, when they realize that things are not so rosy, as he suspected, that for the first time, can I just say: "Hey, my partner (i.e. fluffy) decided, that this agreement does not suit us after all. I'm sorry, but I'm leaving."

I ask you-don't you think it's just for sellers? Does it have its ethics? The seller, who has no doubt already made concrete plans to sell his property, has at least broken hopes-and sometimes much worse.

But that's exactly the approach I propose from time to time as a "safe way" to open homes to many real estate investors across the country.

In fact, many of my colleagues, who teach flipping houses and investing real estate, it also teaches people that it's okay to do business this way. Let me stay away from the crowd and the rude state that I don't approve of-and I don't teach my students-and neither do you.

Are All Unpredictable Clauses?

Almost all contracts have emergency clauses-applicable conditions that must be met in order to be agreement. And the legitimate and proper use of contractual unforeseen events with which I have no problems. It's frequent and gratuitous use these unforeseen events as substitutes for the tasks that I find disturbing.

As a professional real estate investor, you must always be 100% honest with all participants in the transaction. When you sign the contract, do it with honor.

You should offer yourself with the intention of solving the case one way or another. Otherwise, do not close the agreement. If certain circumstances must occur before the conclusion of the contract, submit an offer, but clearly indicate these circumstances in advance. And most importantly, be honest with the seller about your location and ways.

When I was doing business like that, I never lost a deal. And even if I did, I had many other advantageous opportunities.

Even if you put your ethics aside and look at it from a purely selfish point of view, people tend to remember that someone deviates from the agreement and the word circulating. A bad reputation will inevitably catch up with you (yes, even in a big city).

On the other hand, if you sign the honor to experience me again and again learned that you'll be much more successful. In fact, as a result of honoring my contracts, I did not accept my offers in comparison with other, higher offers simply because my name has a decent value. The vendors know I'll do what I say.

Building a reputation has not always been easy.

There was a time when the deal looked like it was going to explode in the face. But every time, when I was able to find a way to honor my word and set the menu, even though it wasn't great deals for me. I also broke on one and made about $ 500 on the other.

But the point is, I fixed them. I don't have to wait for anything else. I went to the street. I was aggressive in finding a way to move things the way they should.

Yes, I have encountered several situations where I couldn't find a wholesale buyer for a particular business. Although my intention when I first started launching homes was exclusively with wholesale deals, I was forced to speak my word in honor of these contracts and settle on the houses myself. So I actually started detox houses.

Believe me, anyone who concentrates on wholesale real estate sales will find themselves in the same position. When you get to this point, if you sign your name with honor, find a way to resolve the matter with integrity, and to repair and return a house or to maintain it, until you find a wholesale buyer (yes, possibly even at a loss).

Bottom...

As an ethical real estate investor, you must sign your name to each contract with honor. Everyone can make an offer, but your name is your name and has value. If you sign contracts without production, Your Name will have little value over time.

Emergency provisions have their place, but you should not use them as a safety net to sign up to deals that you are not sure. You have to sign honestly and always do everything in your power to keep your word.

In the long term your reputation of integrity will bring much more profit and prosperity than any short-term profit, which you can experience as a weasel.

Flipping Houses Ethics: Helping Motivated Sellers

Since then, as a real estate investor in Baltimore in 1998, I was firmly convinced (and have always taught others) that you run your real estate investment business with integrity, and non-negotiable.

In fact, I have written entire chapters in their houses, which continue in the educational material, so that my students know exactly what I think about it.

But a worrying trend of investors in the flipping houses business, who are just too willing to bend the rules-or even break them completely - because of the law has led me to write a series of articles on investing Ethics in the real estate sector - and especially in the field of flipping real estate, which is my specialty.

To this end, I think it would be appropriate to talk about how ethical often navigate dark waters rather than working with motivated sellers when launching real estate.

But before we go there, we should explain exactly what a "motivated seller" is.

Suppliers Vs. Motivated Suppliers

The property seller is someone who wants to sell real estate, while the motivated seller is someone who really needs to sell their property. This house has become a monkey on his back, and are willing to do much more than the average people to get out from under him.

Now, most people usually decide to sell the property for an ordinary reason, because a growing family needs more space, better schools, job opportunities, simple convenience, to "progress" on the East Side, etc.

But when someone really needs to sell, that's another story. Such people usually deal with such things as seizure, transfer of time-sensitive labor, medical expenses, divorce, significant damage, unpaid taxes, establishing the estate, waiting for bankruptcy and others. We all know, or rather, that they were people who found themselves in these unfortunate circumstances.

These people do not just want to sell, they really need it. And they have reached the point that their motivation is large enough to justify the sale of real estate by unconventional, and probably unconventional, means below the market price.

The fact is that motivated sellers are life-blood investing in real estate and home business flipping. To investors in real estate could buy a property at a price low enough to be a good investment, must be the owner of the property generally be in the situation where he has a sale in the sense of discomfort.

Is Flipping case a moral dilemma?

For many, this presents a moral dilemma. Aren't real estate investors really just fueling the desperate situations of people in need? Isn't that immoral?

Good question. But I quickly and unambiguously present to you that the answer is unequivocal "No", but it brings another explanation.

Let's imagine a world for a while without investing in real estate. There are a lot of problems with it, but let's look at one of The Motivated Sellers.

In each of our lives, we find ourselves in a bad state and feel a certain level of despair. It's inevitable. None of us can escape. It's just a question of "when" not " if."

And when there are desperate moments, all we want and need is a solution if we have to find it. And if we find a solution, we will (and should) aggressively promote for relief, provided to us by our desperate situation, if in fact it can be something.

Solution " Problems At Home"

Motivated sellers are people who have a problem with the House. And the more it has to do with it, the more it looks like a time bomb. They seek-no, they really hope and pray for a solution. And you, Mr. or Mrs. Real estate investor, may be the solution.

In a world without real estate investors who will be ready to take a piece of property from the hands of the state immediately, "as is", and with as few questions as possible? In a world without this person, how desperate owners in the world hope to escape from the problem with the house, which of them now sucks life itself?

I say with absolute conviction and integrity, that the relationship of a motivated seller and a real estate entrepreneur is very healthy, mutually beneficial, when practiced with integrity and Justice.

But be careful, experienced investor, that you do not cross the line. It can be too easy.

Houses Against People (People Win)

You know, the impending reason to press the seller, the more motivated tend to solve the problem as quickly and economically as possible.

They're looking for a way out. And if you tell a motivated seller, who must have $ 25,000 in two weeks, that you buy his house within two weeks and he or she leaves with$ 25,000, you can imagine an immediate relief that you need to feel.

For you, this is a business. Your goal is to try to stay without emotions and without connecting to a property or store as much as possible to make bad business decisions.

But the seller is all about the emotion-and especially the relief they feel when the Home problem is no longer on their back.

So even if you do not want to make emotional decisions, you can not forget about the human factor. It's not housekeeping. It's "the businessman."

If you have a contract with a motivated seller, he or she immediately begins to make specific and defined plans based on that transaction, and money and / or relief that will allow. They expect you to keep your commitments because you are a professional in which they have often made a very scary decision to put a lot of trust.

What's he doing now?

What do you do in two weeks if you have not been able to turn their home into a big buyer?

Are you "weasel" with a safeguard clause? This topic what says your partner, who is actually your dog, must approve the purchase?

What happens to the seller now? If you return from the agreement, they can no longer fulfill their obligations and obligations. Their plans were destroyed. He could miss an important opportunity. Perhaps their child will not receive higher education. Maybe they will lose their home and get nothing. They may have to risk their lives and delay the necessary medical procedure.

Personally, I don't know how some people do it. I can't sleep at night signing a contract knowing I'm going to stick to the dealer unless I can find someone else to take him home. The relationship between the motivated seller and the investor in real estate is vital, necessary, if fair use practices for all parties.

But the lesson of the story is that you need to be firmly and absolutely determined to do what you say you will do and not take advantage of motivated sellers. He will always haunt you.

Flipping Houses Ethics: Avoiding Fraud

However, it seems that in recent years it is also an industry that is often better known for unscrupulous investors, shady transactions, and fraudulent activities rather than the economic value that Real Estate Investment brings.

The image we see painted by the media is too often that of the slum lord who keeps his poor tenants under this thumb while enriching himself with their misery. Or it's the fast-talking tycoon who spins his twisted network of House towers, taking advantage of old ladies and making piles of money stealing people's homes.

Although these images are too sensationalized by the media, I am saddened to admit that there is often an unfortunate truth behind them. Also, for moral high fiber real estate investors, it can become too tempting at times to "fib "on the details to get a closed deal especially when the solutions presented are limited and the potential stakes and profits are high.

It is not easy to say "no " to something that seems so little when there are so many things at stake. But be careful, because what seems so little could break your moral fiber, and very well you put in jail to begin with.

How Do You See It In Orange?

Orange suits, that is it. Like what they wear in prison.

We are not afraid of words. What we are talking about here is loan fraud. And many would be successful investors have been courted by how easy it can be to fall, thus turning into rogue investors have now committed loan fraud.

Arrival at home is not illegal or immoral. This problem has been repeatedly addressed by me and others in the field of real estate investment.

But real estate flipping becomes illegal when loan fraud is involved. As a rule, this is since the resale of the returned House is based on inflated valuations, false documents, sales to "straw" buyers representing original sellers or "ghost "secondary loans.

And this is exactly the kind of activity that can (and legitimately must) land in the orange dress, my friend.

But My Boyfriend Ready Told Me He Was Ok!

This problem was aggravated by the fact that several times, when you start investing in real estate, "beginners" do not even realize that they are committing fraud.

Someone else-usually a trusted authority figure-guides you through the process.

They've done it so often that they say, "Oh, believe me, that's okay. We do it all the time. Do not worry about one thing, it's just "understood" in the industry that is fine..."

And like a lamb at the butcher's shop, you offer your moral fiber and your future to sacrifice. This may not seem too much right now, but believe me, it is.

Common Ways To Commit Fraud

Telling a lender that you are buying a home for personal use as opposed to an investment so you can get a lower interest rate or qualify for a higher value loan is a fraud.

Giving a buyer a few thousand dollars so that they have enough funds for a down payment and do not disclose it to the creditor is a fraud.

Marking a purchase contract so that the seller can repay you when you pay for repairs, and not revealing to the creditor is a fraud.

These are just a few scenarios that you will come across regularly.

If loan types say it's good, why isn't it?

When a mortgage broker or lender says it's OK to do something that feels shady, chances are high that they won't be the lender that ultimately finances the deal and collects the payments.

For example, some lenders have already told me that I can give money to my buyers for their down payment when launching homes. I just need my buyer to find a parent to sign a "gift letter" stating that the parent really gave them the money.

Can you believe that? The creditor told me!

Often, a particularly aggressive lender or initiator will simply make the necessary paper tracks simply so that they can conclude the deal and pack the loan into a loan pool, which is then sold to another lender.

Then the lender who buys the loan pool is ultimately the one who has to collect the payments and carries the ultimate risk of dealing with borrowers if the loan defaults.

All this is completely transparent to the investor who sells the property and therefore breaking certain rules seems really harmless, especially when the broker or the initial lender says it is correct to do so.

However, several times the investor is not told the whole story. If so, I suspect that many other transactions would collapse due to the withdrawal of the rehabbers.

As it is, the home flipping investor gets a bad reputation when, in most cases, lenders and mortgage brokers do more damage by facilitating fraudulent transactions.

Once, I sat on the table by a loan agent who asked me to sign a" gift letter" for a buyer. I clarified that since I did not give funds to the buyer, I would not sign the letter. The exact words of the loan agent for me were,

"If you sign this letter, we will settle down next week and you will leave with $ 15,000 on this thing. If you do not, this agreement will fail."

The Right Road Or Highway

I chose to let the case fail. If I can't make the houses the right way, I'd rather not do it at all. You should have the same approach.

Now I'm not saying that all mortgage brokers and lenders commit fraud and investors are never guilty. Thank you for not interpreting it that way.

But I want to make these common pitfalls as clear as possible for the "beginners" who are just starting out in the business of launching homes-those who do not yet have experience but want to do the right thing.

When inexperienced in any field, it is often easy for us to get lost and do unethical things by accident simply because an authority figure has quietly appeased our concerns.

Honestly, sometimes it is very difficult to do the right thing, especially when no one is watching. I'm not superhuman. Temptation is a common denominator for all of us, especially when dollar signs are important. And they can be in this business.

But it is this flipping of houses with integrity is to do the right thing, even when no one looks. And believe me, in the long run, doing the right thing always pays off.

Is Flipping Houses Legal?

"I recently heard the news of investors who went to prison because they were coming home. Is he tearing down the law houses?"

The reason this problem continues to come has a lot to do with the work that the media continues to do in misrepresenting the real estate investment industry. Let me get this straight.

First of all, let me be very clear. The concept of real estate flipping is not illegal. There is absolutely nothing wrong with buying a house at a price, and then selling it at a higher price.

And that's exactly what "flipping "is - just another way of saying "buy, then sell."

Think about this: if I owned a lot of cars, I would buy cars at a wholesale price and then sell them to end users for a higher retail price. And I hope to make a profit in the process, right? Do you think I'd do something wrong by "throwing cars" like that? Of course not-it is done every day.

And if I owned a hardware store, I would have" returned" everything from Hammers to nails to my clients, right?

Understand that what we are talking about here is essentially capitalism and our economy depends on it. This is a normal way of life for all of us in US. Companies "return" goods and services to us, which we pay in turn. And the profit they receive is not considered immoral.

So, what about the "turnaround scandals" we hear so much about in the media?

To put it simply, the launch of real estate becomes illegal only when fraud is involved. And when that happens, it's usually that resale is based on inflated valuations, fake documents, sales to "straw" buyers representing original sellers or "ghost "side loans.

Loan fraud is illegal. But buying and selling houses for profit is absolutely not. In fact, there's also no ethical problem if your buyer wanted to pay you much more than market value, as long as he doesn't lie about value or defraud buyers or lenders.

Most lenders do not lend more than one property worth it. However, if your buyers have the means to pay you, and the property is worth it, then this is their choice, clear and simple. And no law is broken.

Reversal...Video games?

For a little more clarity on this, let's spend a moment in the video game industry. Have you noticed that when the latest generation of game system is released, people will pay crazy, crazy amounts of money just to get their hands on one the day you launch?

In fact, when the Sony PlayStation 3® was released in November 2006, the retail value was about $ 600. But as often happens these days with high-end gaming systems, the initial supply of PS3 was much lower than its immediate demand, and only a handful of people managed to get their hands on one the day it launched.

The hype-up demand for these gaming systems is intriguing in itself. But even more interesting is the fact that most people who bought a unit on launch day were not even interested in keeping them. Instead, they went straight to the online auction arena and let the market do this.

On launch day, these $ 600 gaming systems were "returned" to eBay for staggering returns - from $ 3,000 to $ 10,000 from the hungry masses of Game buyers.

Was it illegal? Immoral or immoral? No, no and no.

What were these systems really worth? Well, the price of the sticker was about $ 600. But the market spoke and determined the value of the excess of four figures.

Do hungry eBay buyers know they were paying a much higher price than the sellers had just paid for the same system at their best local purchase? Absolutely, and they have no cure.

For buyers on launch day, the value of having a gaming system as quickly as possible was more important to them than the radical price increase.

The actual value is determined by what the honest and open market is willing to pay rather than the "sticker price" or valuation value.

To come back to this point, as I said, what people typically call "illegal real estate flipping" is actually mortgage fraud. But the media have for some reason, in its glorious ignorance, hijacked the term "flipping" as the password to describe these scams.

This is a sad disservice to a world of honest and ethical real estate investors who legitimately return homes for a living.

As a result, the media have given big trend reversal and real estate invest a bad reputation in general, because they do not focus on the real problem. The real problem with "illegal flipping" is when investors, mortgage brokers, loan agents, experts, etc. they come together to fabricate a better image of a buyer or a property of a creditor than it actually exists. Put another way, they lie.

They do things like creating W-2 fakes, creating payroll stubs, inflating valuations, donating down payment, writing letters of credit, etc...

People who do this deserve to go to jail. But it is not the same as returning property.

Real estate investors who are engaged in the legitimate business of launching homes (either as "wholesalers" or "fix-and-flip" rehabilitation investors) actually play a key (and underappreciated) role in stimulating our economy. And having them unfairly classified as "immoral" or "illegal" just because they invest in time-bound real estate flipping is sad.

The bottom line is, if you buy a property below market value, sell it for more and make a profit - and if you do it honestly, ethically and without committing any fraud on the loans, then you are not doing anything illegal. You have nothing to worry about.

Does Flipping Houses Break the Law?

Flipping houses are also commonly referred to as integral houses. This simply means acquiring a property at a lower price and selling it at a higher price to make a profit.

Just like any other business, returning homes involves buying low-rise homes and then selling high. Since real estate transactions can become complicated, real estate investment activity is poorly understood. And, of course, some real estate investors weren't honest, so they got into trouble.

Is it illegal to return houses?

First of all, do not take this article as legal advice; you should always consult your lawyer. Real estate investors who get into legal trouble usually break the law one way or another.

What does it mean to return the houses? Although the definition above means buy low and then sell high, the details of the transaction may vary, leading to misunderstandings. We will explore the legality of each method.

1) Contract assignment

The award of the contract means that you identify a home below market value, you contract it, and then assign that contract to a commission to a wholesale investor or buyer.

In this case, what you sell the right to buy the house, but you do not actually sell the house.

You go home with an allowance fee at the end.

It's the easiest way to turn houses around. Note that you do not represent anyone, or even own the property at any time during the transaction. He simply secures a house under contract, then sells this contract right to close.

2) Simultaneous closure

Simultaneous closure involves contracting the home, identifying a wholesale buyer, buying it and selling the home to the buyer.

Both transactions take place on the same closing table, one where you buy and the other where you sell. So you own the house for a few minutes before selling it.

There are two sets of closing fees and you walk home with the difference between the purchase price and the sale price.

3) Purchase, fixing and sale

Although flipping houses generally do not fit this description, some people buy a house, fix it, and then sell it for profit.

There is nothing wrong with that, just buy low, improve the value, then the high selling.

What can go wrong in flipping houses?

1) Representing a third party without a license

Returning homes never involves representing another person in the transaction. You sell the right to buy the property, or you buy the property, and then sell it for a profit.

A real estate agent represents a buyer or seller and leaves with a commission. To do this, a license is required.

2) Mortgage fraud

Of course, it is illegal to commit mortgage fraud. No matter what type of transaction is involved, it will certainly get you into trouble.

3) Don't tell the truth

When buying houses from motivated sellers, it is crucial to be very clear and in particular let them know exactly how you manage the sale. All they need to know is how much they get according to your agreement and when the agreement will be reached.

I like to go further and let them know exactly how I handle the transaction, so if there is a delay, they understand why.

As long as you are clear and never distort anything, then you have nothing to fear.

The Philosophy of Flipping Houses

There is a "philosophy" for almost everything. And the case of flipping houses is no exception. Wait a second. Isn't philosophy a matter of thought? Speculation?

In fact, it is. Philosophy comes from an old Greek word meaning "love for wisdom." But it's much more than that. Philosophy is the whole branch of science that deals with knowledge, reality and existence. And philosophers do exactly what philosophy implies, which is ... Think. We can find clear links between the practical and practical activity of turnaround houses and the esoteric science of philosophy. More than you think.

Just as turning houses can be compared to physics or art because business has things that relate directly to these subjects, upside-down houses can be linked to philosophy. Follow me here if you like...

Philosophy tries to understand what is mysterious. If the subject is simple, easy and obvious, it is likely that philosophical thinkers do not think, or talk about it. They prefer difficult themes. They ask questions, challenging questions, and then see who can answer. Then they challenge those answers.

What is important in life? Why is this important? Who decides what is and is not? What are moral norms and why are they perceived differently by different people? How do I know I know something? How do I know if what I think I know is reality? Or just my imagination?

You can understand why philosophers don't do much in a work day.

But... there is actually value in what these people do. Think. (Okay, it was philosophical) When you approach turning houses, how do you see it? Why are you doing this instead of anything else? After all, everyone has the same 24 hours a day. No one has more. No one understands less. So we neglect to do things that could be done if we did not look for houses to return. And that means we make value judgments about our time. And determining what is precious is a way of thinking. And that kind of thinking is... Philosophy.

There is also a "philosophy" about how we approach business. It is considered to repair the house as the real meat of the turning houses. Another sees marketing as the most vital phase. And another sees the sales trade to be the biggest battle. You might look to return homes as a great use of your gifts to give back to your neighbor in better neighborhoods and better lives. Or you might see business as the best way to provide to those you love, whether it's your favorite job or not. Or, you might see the company as the funniest you could have and still get paid.

It doesn't matter. These are all philosophies. They are all ways to visually display the business. And they all influence the way everyone does their job. So when you think, and especially philosophically, think about how your thinking affects your business.

How to Start Flipping Houses

Mirror or "flipping" homes always has and will always be a very profitable way to make money until you go about it properly.

There are a lot of people who have become very rich by running houses. However, there are definitely different ways to do this and the way you choose will have a big impact on how successful you will be when you do it.

Here are some very useful tips to consider when you decide to enter into the practice of returning homes and if you follow them, your chances of succeeding and making a profit will be much better:

- Avoid unnecessary expenses - Make sure you spend as little as possible on renovations, focus your efforts on the kitchen and bathrooms as these are what will have a considerable impact on any sale.

- Do it right the first time - Try to do it always from the beginning, it will help you avoid wasting money by having to do things. Always keep in mind the safety of the potential buyer and never use mistreatment.

- Keep your budget - Always have a budget on what you are willing to spend on renovations and keep it.

- Don't try to solve what you don't need - Focus your contribution on those things you really feel need attention and avoid wasting money to fix things in the house that already work.

- Keep in mind the area and house prices - It does not help to renovate a home from the potential price range of the area in which it is located. Always keep in mind the potential sale price for the area.

- Keep time limits - Always know how much time you are willing to spend around the house before you want to return, remember, time is money.

Flipping homes can be a lot of fun and generate a big income, if you use these tips correctly, you should be able to see the profits very soon. Always take the time to invest in yourself and make sure you've done your homework before buying a property for turnaround purposes.

The Best Cities For Flipping Houses

When you decide that you start throwing houses, one of the main questions you have in mind should be where you carry out your activities. After all, as anyone who has had years of relationships with the real estate market will be able to treat you, attitude is very important when it comes to buying and selling real estate, both from the point of view of housing demand and prices, which you can pay for the property.

This means that some markets will naturally be stronger than others, so it's a good idea to know where to start before buying. Here we will see some of the best cities to return home to the current market.

Memphis, TN

Memphis is one of the most famous cities in the United States, but according to recent statistics it is also one of the best when it comes to throwing home. In 2015, the city has so far successfully overturned about 250 homes, one of the highest in the United States.

Even better is, on average, a pinball House about $ 50,000 in revenue on each house sold, with an average purchase price of approximately $ 100,000, while the average sales price was just over$150,000. Given the cost of renovations, this could likely mean about a $ 20-25. 000 profit for each home returned to the city.

Our services

Baltimore-Towson has numbers very similar to Memphis, statistics suggest that 258 homes were returned to the city in the first quarter of the year. However, the city stands out from the rest of the list because of the huge return on investment offered by each returned property.

The average purchase price of a house in 2015 was about $ 125,000, but the average sale price reached a remarkable $ 243,000. There is simply no cheaper market in the country today is for people who want to make more money from returning home, but beware that it will be a very busy market, because more and more people are aware of the potential that it offers.

Ocala, FL

Ocala is a great city to start flip a home business because the initial prices for the property are relatively low and there is a good chance that you will see a return on fixed investment in this area. So if your budget isn't huge, it could be the perfect place to start.

The average purchase price in the city is around $ 51,000, with sales prices hovering around the $ 90,000 area. Although this sales price is not huge compared to other areas, it still accounts for nearly $ 40,000 in revenue from each sale. Some homes sold in Ocala could mean you are able to save the money needed to work in a thriving city. The only problem you will face is that there is not a large number of goods on the market, only 69 returned in the first quarter of 201

Basic Steps to Flipping Houses For Profit

There has been a lot of attention lately focusing on launching for-profit real estate. Many people have heard about this, but few understand it and how to find suitable properties to return. Many of you have probably heard of this strategy of flipping homes by watching TV or hearing ads on the radio. If you do not, then this article should help you understand the pros and cons of flipping houses and what to look for. While there are some people who may have had negative experiences with this strategy to make money due to business bad or less than perfect job done by the entrepreneurs, shady, by following the tips here, it will return to profit in the right way and avoiding all the negative aspects of having your head and shoulders right.

One of the most important aspects of cashing in on the real estate investment market is finding a suitable location. You've probably heard this many times before, but it couldn't be further from the truth that location is the most important aspect of valuing any property. For a flip to succeed a house must be in a prime location. It's a good idea to check local newspapers in your area for homes that move relatively well in a specific neighborhood. This will allow you to clear a good property reversal.

In addition to finding a good location, it is also important to look for properties that require only minor repairs and small cosmetic touches to bring them on a par. This is very important because you do not want to tie precious money and time to renovate a property. If you are tied to a property because of the amount of work that needs to be done for this, you will probably lose money. This is where you could be smart and order a home check. The amount of money spent on a good home inspection will certainly pay you later and could save you a fortune in time and money. An inspection can reveal hidden problems within the property and allow you to adjust the auction to cover the cost of repair.

Finding a good entrepreneur can easily make or break a deal. It is very important to communicate directly with your entrepreneur that time is essential when launching the property for profit. Look for an entrepreneur who has a good reputation and has experience with this type of work. Find out from your local real estate offices about various contractors. Real estate agents can be a great source of information. Once you find a reliable contractor, it is important to convey the speed and production needs. Being ahead and knowing what to expect from each other is the key to a successful business relationship.

Flipping houses can be a very profitable business if done correctly and with the appropriate knowledge. Passing the basic steps above is a must to succeed in this venture. You will need to have everything in order and a vivacity of mind ready to negotiate for the best deals. Working well with a team, maintaining a positive attitude and being experienced in the basic skills of turning at home is a must. If you focus on the important tips included here and apply this knowledge, you will be an expert in no time and will be seriously rewarded.

Secrets of Flipping Houses For A Quick Profit

Buying cheap real estate, quickly improving it and selling it right after it is a proven way to earn money quickly. This is called House turning, and the current economic crisis means that there are a number of cheap homes that you can buy and renovate-if you feel you have a knack for d-I-Y repairs and home painting.

Here are some tips to help you get started with flipping homes for quick profit:

Look for real opportunities. Home flipping is all about buying a dirty home-cheaply, doing some cosmetic repairs, and then reselling the property for a healthy profit.

If you are not sure whether to buy real estate or not, take someone with you who has experience in building and building houses. Otherwise, what you think is a deal could end up costing you a fortune in repairs or even reconstruction. Remember, flipping homes is to spend as little as possible on the renovation as possible.

Make sure that if you plan to go into flipping homes, you get your mortgage pre approved. This way you will know exactly what you can afford and you will be able to negotiate accordingly.

Do your research. If you want to start throwing houses in a particular area, find out what the average prices are, then you can buy low and sell at least the average.

When you do the home flipping, you want to do most of the repair and renovation work yourself-this way you can reduce costs, and make a bigger profit when you sell. The less you have to hire entrepreneurs, the more money you will earn when you sell.

If you're trying to get into the house by throwing, there are two things you need to avoid like plague-houses with plumbing problems, and those with power outages. These are two of the most expensive to solve and will eat into your profits before you know it.

As you can see, there's not much to consider when you start throwing houses. Therefore, if you have some money, or can access the financing, you might consider making some extra money from the real estate market as you recover from the recession.

Succeeding in Flipping Houses

Managing to go home and bring big profits is one of the current trends in the real estate world these days. This means buying a house at a low price or perhaps a neglected house and selling it quickly at a higher market value. Successful return of houses can be possible if you give him a lot of effort and follow all the necessary details with this business. To help you get started here are some good tips that would make room for you to succeed in returning homes.

The first thing you want to look at is that you know everything about the house you are buying. You need to see and evaluate what type or type of House is selling quickly, what are the needs of this particular community, you can also try to start with the average type of houses for the average type of families. Depending on the destination area, you should also evaluate the average cost of houses in this area. You do not want to overpay this house and make it a longer process for sale.

Many will focus on one problem aesthetically at home, but this is not necessary. This is not what the intuition of being able to launch houses is all about. Keep in mind that houses with aesthetic problems or simply bad houses could work in your real estate niche, but you can return a perfectly beautiful house that is at market price. Faded, dull or fragile colors, tall grasses or ruined Gardens, stinky houses, holes on the wall, stains on the carpet, window treatments are just some of the aesthetic problems you are looking for in a home. These aesthetic problems are an easy-to-solve home that can be sold for minimal profit to the next buyer.

Stay away from major renovations. Changing the entire roof, major plumbing issues and repairs, great electrical doing more, Wall renovations and tastes are the things you wanted to avoid. Besides the fact that it will eat your budget, these things take longer to complete the incompatibility with your main goal is to get things moving as fast as possible.

Finally, separating your personal money from your business money will certainly help you succeed in returning home. The most strategic way is to get a loan to finance the renovation of the House. By following this technique, you will tend to have more control over your budget and avoid mixing up your personal company finances.

Now that you know some tricks to be able to knock down houses, do your best and do your research and make sure that you end up with a wonderful job that will bring you profits.

Fixing and Flipping Houses For Profit - How Much to Renovate?

Any investor who wants to make money by returning homes must understand what to repair, renovate or improve and what to leave alone. It can be a difficult balance. If you improve the house too much, it can be difficult to make a profit when selling because the house is too expensive for the neighborhood. On the other hand, if you improve too little, you may not be able to get the price you wanted, because the value added to the property was not enough to justify your price. Here are some tips to determine the appropriate level of improvement for your home's vibrations.

Your search starts before you even find a property you want. Go to as many open doors as possible, in the neighborhoods where you plan to buy. Take a notebook with you and use it to record your observations and ideas. What you are going to do is evaluate the type of services that are typical for the neighborhood. This will let you know what level of renovation you need to apply to your home.

You need to familiarize yourself with the types of features common to most of the best homes. You will gather a lot of ideas to improve your vibration at home and how much money to spend to do it.

Pay attention to the specific parts to see what quality of materials is standard. While renovations should always be quality work, you have plenty of room for man oeuvre in the types of materials you use. For a modest neighborhood, stick to cheaper (but still quality) floors, suspended ceilings, etc. On the other hand, if your home is in a rich or quickly improve the neighborhood, you can choose several luxurious materials that reflect the more sophisticated tastes of the potential buyer.

Ask your realtor what services the most expensive homes that have recently sold in the neighborhood have. So, make sure the home you are buying has these features or include them in your home renovation plans.

Always keep your renovations in line with what the buyer expects. It is a mistake to improve your home far beyond the standards of other homes in the neighborhood. The best strategy is to make your house flip just a little better than the most beautiful house recently sold.

Restructuring to avoid

There are some renovations that, as a real estate investor, you really don't want to do. They are too expensive and take too much time, without a sufficient return on investment. For example, do not buy a house that needs additional measures to put it on a par with the most beautiful houses in the neighborhood.

If you want to knock down an interior wall to open the space, that's fine. But when you decide to add the footprint of the house, you will need a new roof and foundation for additional rooms. And for this kind of renovation you will need architectural plans, engineering plans, permits and more time and money than it is worth. Stick to home improvements that are simple and cost effective.

An improvement that adds a special appeal

If you need something to increase the perceived value of your home, consider building a wooden bridge in the backyard.

A bouquet is relatively inexpensive, but it has a great emotional appeal to the owner of the House.

Bridges are associated with outdoor relaxation and comfort, fun, family barbecue and other positive events.

Most buyers like them. You will find that this feature adds much more value to the home than it costs.

Flipping Houses and Lease Purchase Agreement

Flipping homes is a good way to make quick money for real estate investors.

You need to know some basic concepts and strategies before you start throwing houses and making money out of it.

This study can prevent you from suffering heavy losses that are involved in real estate investments.

What is real estate investment and Home launch?

Real estate investments and flipping houses are closely related.

People involved in real estate investments today make a huge amount of money by throwing houses.

Returning homes is simply buying a property and reselling it quickly at higher rates.

For experienced investors, it is not a difficult task to find a buyer who is interested in buying the goods they sell.

But if you are a beginner, you may encounter some difficulties. Understanding some basic concepts can help you.

- Always study your market so that you make a fast and profitable business.

- Prepare your finances so that you can conclude the deal profitably.

- Get help from the contract and forms that are available to assist you in real estate investment and Home launch.

- Market your properties and homes you sell, based on your location and market conditions.

- Quickly find the qualified buyer so you can close the deal early.

- Learn all the legal concepts and paperwork involved.

Flipping houses and buying rentals

Renting buying or leasing is a great way to attract more buyers to your property. Even if it is more profitable for buyers, it will help you avoid huge losses.

Leasing is a better option to attract buyers, who do not have enough money to buy a house. They can take the help of the rental option and get from their dream home to rent at home.

According to this, they must pay a certain amount of fixed money to the seller as a down payment, and then a fixed monthly rent for the property they use.

Leasing is a contract between buyers and sellers for the fixed time interval. After they have it the case. This is in favor of the buyer, and they have the right to buy the house after this period of time.

Even in the event that the buyer is not interested or find that it is not a good deal for them, they can return the deal.

The rental purchase is therefore a great way by which investors can find interested buyers quickly and easily.

The Rules of Flipping Houses

The number one rule when it comes to your career in flipping houses, it is not allowing anyone to convince you that it's illegal or immoral. Neither! Domestic fins meet the service they so desperately need in the communities they invest in. Come to the aid of people who need and / or want to sell their homes, but not on the conventional market. Maybe they are in a hurry to move, or maybe the house requires too much work. A home pinball machine provides these people with the money and speed they need to leave their current home. Then flipper House makes the wrong house beautiful and adds value to its surroundings.

Another rule of life in this business is to make money when you buy a house, not when you sell it. You will get your profit from the discount you get from its fair market value. As we have said, usually sellers for the domestic flipping market must sell quickly and for as much money as they can get for it. You may not be their ideal buyer, but you can be their sole buyer. Therefore, you can get it at an exceptional price. You would buy a house at a discount on its own value. So, it's going to be a great investment for you.

Another rule that you should spend in a world flipping home is to be picky (at least with the first offers) and keep things simple. If the House needs too much work, it will not be an advantage for you to buy it. In this case, it will cost you more money than you want. Whether you estimate restructuring costs for you will be, you should consider that when you make an offer for his seller.

Another rule is rather a general strategic plan for yourself when starting a home. Take advantage of all tax deductions allowed by the law. Talk to your accountant about it. Can inform you of any tax breaks that fully apply to you of the law and regulations governing the real estate investment. Then follow the accounting advice. Plus, it would be helpful for him to keep a great budget. Make sure that you have a sufficient record of all expenses and income of all investment real estate. This will allow your accountant to identify deductions that you can and cannot accept very easily.

For more information about other rules for flipping home, check out your favorite search engines on the internet. Type: "rules for returning home."Your search will get you a lot of useful information. Yeah, you can break houses, too.

Wholesaling Real Estate Vs Rehabbing and Flipping Houses

Why are the most successful professionals investing in real estate holding wholesale against rehabbing and launching reality-style homes?

Many may not even realize the difference in wholesale compared to repairing and launching houses, but it's great. So, what is different and what is better for today's real estate investors?

Wholesale vs Home repair and rotation

Flipping homes is a general category that actually includes several different real estate investment strategies, including rehabilitation and other home sales like those reality shows, as well as truth, wholesale, and launching real estate contracts.

Real estate wholesalers will find discounted real estate and instantly turn them for quick cash. Sometimes they buy and sell them, or often simply take advantage of the current conclusion or assign their contracts for an interesting fee. They rarely do any work at these properties and, while some are sold at retail, many home buyers are passed on to other investors who will make repairs, and then keep them as retail or public rentals.

Dangers of rehabilitation and sales houses

Reality television has made repairing and launching homes an incredibly popular pastime.

While it certainly holds profits for the experienced real estate investor, helps rejuvenate communities and can be a lot of fun, it can also be a money-losing nightmare and has certainly bankrupt its fair share of newbie investors.

The biggest problem is that at heart this is a speculative strategy of investing in real estate.

Investors who are great at doing homework and due diligence, understanding the values of construction and home, and invested in their training, you can get a good idea of what they can sell and minimize risks, but still rely on finding a buyer who will pay them what they hoped after the House goes well.

Of course, unfortunately, it does not always work this way, and many new investors who rush into this strategy with a passion quickly find themselves in the head, exploit funds and with an unfinished property that you can not sell, refinance or rent.

Even in the best case is often not the most advantageous strategies to invest in real estate, and then there are additional requirements for a hard cash advance, the risks of keeping the Times and all those bad additional costs for repairs are found once repairs have begun.

Advantages of Wholesale vs. Real Estate repair and flipping

In contrast, those who stick to straight Wholesale are able to use 100% of their investment, so virtually no exposure to personal losses and you won't have to roll up your sleeves on weekends to try and fix what the contractor has left undone.

It's about letting someone else take big risks and do a hard job, while often taking equal or higher net profits.

Wholesalers also generally turn around their homes and convert their offers into cash in a few days, it means a quick succession of pay and the potential to do a lot more trades per month, or a year, than those who spend weeks or months laying at home and then marketing.

The increase in the demand for investment properties today also means wholesalers are blessed with a growing market with a large number of final buyers who essentially pre-order these homes, locking in profits for the wholesaler before the property is even bought.

New investors should also realize that unlike some wholesale misconceptions this is not a small gig.

This can be done part - time for a few hours a week, although it is also easily scalable and has earned an additional excess of $1 million a month.

Working in Real Estate - Jobs Like Flipping Houses

If you are looking to decide between a career in real estate or starting with Real Estate Jobs like launching homes for investors, you should thoroughly research the real estate market and see if you have the tenacity. Working in real estate requires good communication and organizational skills. They are day-to-day people and constantly sell themselves.

Many people glorify the profession by focusing solely on the material aspects that the Great commission controls and works on the ground; this is just a snapshot of what work in real estate is like. It takes time, effort, drive all day in several hours to welcome your customers and patience with people who do not know exactly what they want. All this goes without glamour and this big gain comes only after long days tired of patience and willingness to work beyond what you really want on these beautiful sunny days.

Most real estate careers require a real estate license, while jobs like flipping homes do not require a license, but a lot of time and effort. Flipping requires you to be disciplined, organized and personality to adapt to different environments and people. Not everyone you meet will be courteous and polite and many will possess the opposite traits. This does not mean that you should not jump into a career by throwing houses.

Flip houses really don't require any credit; it's good to have a credit + as it allows you to trade more freely and open more doors and opportunities, but good credit is not a mandatory requirement.

Starting, you might consider having money saved. Beginners have a hard time persuading creditor to give up payments; you'll be in a better position once you complete certain transactions.

If you want to work for a real estate investor by spotting throw opportunities for them, go ahead with caution. This can be illegal in many states. Many states do not allow anyone to be compensated for helping someone locate real estate unless you are authorized. Now, you can overcome this problem by focusing on one thing to help an investor sift through all the information he needs, such as checking land and tax valuation records. This type of work you can be compensated without fear of restrictions of any state.

To successfully work for a real estate investor by providing information for the launch property, you need to conduct thorough research on random information and learn everything about the market that interests the investor. This will reduce your search and become more effective in collecting your information.

So if you start a new career working in real estate or you decide that you just want to start with a job throwing houses, you can learn the ropes of the craft and quickly climb the ranks.

Investing in Real Estate – The Flipping Houses Game

Real estate and land have long been solid investment opportunities for those who learn about them and learn the best way to get a return on investment. For some time now, the so-called "overthrown houses" movement has been popular. Is this a really strong investment potential? The answer to this question is yes and no. There are a few factors to consider that can be individual for each investment opportunity and the investor himself. These factors include the condition of the property, the location of the property and the investor's ability to make repairs and improvements.

In some cases, the flipping game is very profitable. These are cases where some or all of the following circumstances occur:

Location - the property or house is in an area that is relatively high in demand as a popular neighborhood or a busy street.

Condition-the property is recoverable within a reasonable budget that will allow the investor to buy the property, improve the property and sell the house at a reasonable market value and get a profit.

Cost the purchase price of a house that needs renovation must be less than the market value of the House.

Ability to solve - the above two factors are important, but this is perhaps the most important. If the investor has the skills or ties to those who have the skills to perform repairs and improvements at a lower than average cost, the return can be significant. The investor who is best placed to make money from a home flipping situation is one who is an entrepreneur or other expert. This type of person can make a lot of improvements on their own or know those who can make improvements at a low rate.

Investing in a flip home is something that can lead to a solid return, but only if the investor knows their way around the world, restructuring, and knows how to get things improved without breaking the bank so to speak. The average person without Housing Improvement skills is not likely to see a good return on such an investment, as they will have to pay for all the improvements and then shift those costs over the selling price. This sometimes makes the selling price too much above the market value in this case. For more information on investments in investment opportunities usually or normally not found in the market.

Rehabbing Ugly Houses Will Give You Beautiful Profits

Owning a home may be the American dream, but many people dream of making money in real estate.

We all read stories about someone who made millions in real estate.

The fact is that many people live their dreams by buying bad houses and then selling them weeks or a few months later-often for good profits.

But how are some people able to do this, sometimes even beginners?

It is not surprising, there are some rules to follow. And the more attention you pay to the rules, the better the chances of earning serious money.

I made my real estate debut several years ago by "flipping" houses. What is flipping at home?

Returning a home is the process of buying a home that needs repairs, at a price well below market value, quickly adding value by making the necessary repairs to get the house to market standards, and then selling the house for a profit.

And you do it using little or no of your money. Sounds pretty easy, doesn't it?

But flipping through the houses is not the way to get rich quickly, and this is certainly not for everyone.

Here are some rules to follow if you decide that you want to make money by investing in real estate, including by launching homes.

1. **Use The Formula.** Buying the wrong house at the right price is essential to make a profit. You actually make your profits when you buy the House, not when you sell it. You realize your profit when you sell it. Remember that what you get for your home after repairing will depend on what similar properties are selling in the area. It will have nothing to do with what you spent on repairing the House.

The following formula worked well for me and for you:

<u>**A**. determines the "value after repair" (ARV) of the home you plan to purchase</u>. In general, you can determine the ARV by obtaining a list of comparable sales ("comps") in the area of a realtor. If you rely on comps, make sure you get the actual selling price of the homes sold and not the list price. Determining the likely selling price of your home is the starting point.

B. <u>subtract the total cost from the selling price:</u>

- Closing fees
- Borrowing costs
- Document preparation costs
- Owner insurance
- Title of the policy
- Repair costs
- Interest on the loan
- Property taxes
- Sales Commissions
- Other expenditure

You want to project costs according to four major categories.

Purchase, repair, transportation or possession and sale. After determining the estimated costs of the four categories, subtract the total costs from the selling price.

C. once you subtract the costs from your expected selling price, you will generate your estimated profit.

You will have to decide how much of a profit you want to make on the deal to make it worth it.

When you determine the desired result, you will have the highest price you want to pay for the House.

If you constantly use the formula, you will make better and faster decisions about a potential bad home. Always start with the value after repaired and then work your way through the costs to calculate the desired profit.

Also, do not let your emotions get away from you and make a decision about the pants that you will later regret. If the figures do not add up depending on the desired profit, go ahead. Be patient.

2. He Works With An Experienced Realtor. I find this amazing, but too many investors think that all realtors are created equal. That's not true. If your goal is to buy dilapidated homes, then you need to find a realtor specializing in foreclosures, HUD properties, etc. in fact I had a fairly inexperienced investor tell me that he thought any realtor could help him achieve his goal. It's possible, but probably not. To get the right result, you need to go to the right realtor.

Doctors are doctors, but some have their own specialty. If you have a severe case of flu, would you go to a doctor to help you overcome your misery? For example, would you go to a gynecologist? Of course not. So why go to a realtor to help you find the distressed property? You get it.

3. Use The Lever. Rightly called "leverage, we recommend that you take full advantage of leverage, because it is the key to wealth in real estate investment. Leverage is the use of borrowed money to increase profits when buying a bad home. Using little or no of your money to buy more homes allows you to make a good profit on other people's money.

Even if your goal should be to buy goods for thousands below its value, and sometimes you can buy without money down, it is important to understand that does not necessarily mean that the seller does not receive money at the close. Rather, it means that there is little or no money out of your pocket to do the trick.

Some investors think there is something wrong with using someone else's money to buy homes. Well, for most working families, leverage not only provides them with a roof over their heads and extraordinary tax breaks, but also the best investment they will ever make.

Most real estate investors work hard at home flipping, have a long-term plan and stick to it. You can certainly narrow your way to achieving your financial goals by using leverage.

4. Use Psychology. When repairing the house, let psychology guide you. You don't have the love of the House. Your potential buyer must, like her. Remember, you will not live in the house, so do not overdo it with repairs. If you have carefully defined your niche market, you will know their likes and dislikes. Make the right repairs to get the house to market standards, then stop and put a "For Sale" sign on it. I've talked to new investors who frankly admit to doing too much at home, but they couldn't help themselves because they didn't like the way it looked. Making too much for a house is no different from taking your money and throwing it out the car window. Either way, you lose.

There is almost no other business that allows you to buy bad houses and make good profits with almost all of your money in a short time. It is well known that more millionaires have made their fortune in real estate than in any other business. So, what are you waiting for? Rehabbing ugly homes can give you good profits.

Flip Houses Online

Nowadays, real estate market always changes its demand and supply quickly. While some people want to sell their home quickly, the other will immediately buy the House. For you, this is a good chance, because you can earn a lot of money from change.

But the efficiency is low. If you want to ensure your high success rate, it is better to use the internet and learn how to return homes online.

Item 1

Evaluate your potential property. There is no guarantee in real estate. However, if your property meets certain requirements, you can make an informed estimate of how investors will react. For example, a property must have a fair amount of investor capital to justify the sale. Also, if the property needs repairs, you should get estimates for these and comparable prices on other homes in the area. Once everything is taken into account, investors will always want to see significant profit potential in the end. For example, a house that values $ 100,000 and needs $ 20,000 in repairs will not be a good candidate if the seller wants $ 70,000 for it, as it leaves the investor with only about 10 percent of the equity after completing the repairs. Of course, you should consult a financial professional for help in determining whether a property is viable.

Item 2

Take the property under contract. If you determine that the property is worth trying to return, get it under contract. Your contract should allow you to assign the contract to another investor and protect yourself in the event that the property does not return so as not to get stuck with the House. You can find contracts for this kind of thing online, or you can hire a lawyer to create one for you (see the resources below). You should never use a contract that has not been approved by your lawyer.

Item 3

Build a page on your blog with property details. Once you have the property under contract, build a blog page dedicated to that property.

It should include all the details you know and solve all the problems that investors may have, like why you don't keep the property to yourself if it's a good deal.

This particular problem is easily solved by pointing out that you simply do not like owning a property, but prefer to come back because it's easier, even if a long-term investor earns much more money.

Item 4

Inform your email list of investors that you have a property. Send your list of real estate investors an email directing them to your blog page where they can learn all about this property opportunity.

Let them know how to get in touch with you if they are interested in doing a job.

Do not give them contact information for the seller, or you may find yourself excluded from the transaction.

Item 5

Select the most promising investor and work with her to make the deal.

You can do the due diligence work yourself or be part of the investor's responsibility.

Before the contracts are signed, you must do everything again with your lawyer to make sure that everything is written correctly.

Item 6

Take your share and withdraw from the transaction.

As a rule, you will receive your cut at the end of the transaction.

Remember, once you sign the documents, it is no longer your business, so you do not need field calls or help with due diligence, unless your contract states so.

Understanding Confusing Contracts

Everyone can manage to get home, but it can take patience and time to understand confusing contracts, especially for the beginner pinball player.

Articles and blogs on the internet tell you how easy it is to go home, but to really succeed, you need to understand by launching houses and contracts. There is no longer a type of vibration, but more and more real estate investors are opting for an options contract.

The owner agrees to sell his property to a buyer for a price. They create a contract, but the buyer has the opportunity to sell to another buyer at the predetermined price that the owner requires. The buyer does not make promises, and the owner wants only the asking price. Because of this type of contract to become executive, in most states, the buyer must give the owner a certain type of tax. It's just to make the contract enforceable. This is not a deposit for the purchase of the house or any kind of serious money and can not be credited on the purchase price. It does not have to be a certain amount or percentage of the asking price; only an acceptable value for the owner. The owner gets to keep these expenses or not you decide to go through the contract.

Once you have a contract on the house now, you can sell your option to another interested party-who wants to buy the House. You must never take possession of the house; you must not participate in any settlement or title deed on your behalf.

An example of flipping houses and understanding contracts;

You approach an owner who wants to sell his house for $150,000. You really do not have money for a large down payment or settlement, so ask the owner if he would be interested in selling the house in the next 6 months. He says yes, so you're trying to negotiate a contract.

You tell the owner that you will give him $ 1,000 if he signs a contract agreeing to sell the house within the next 6 months for its asking price of $150,000. Explain that the $ 1,000 you can keep for a fee just to venture into this business. The owner agrees.

Some clauses of the contract give you the opportunity to buy the house, but you have the right to assign your option to another buyer; you are not really obliged to buy the House.

Once the fees are given to the owner and the contract signed, you start looking for an investor to buy the home at the owner's asking price of $150,000 plus the fair market price that can put the real value of the home at perhaps$175,000. At the end of the day when the sale of the House.

Tax Reporting for Flipping Houses

Are you coming home? Then it is better to pay taxes; especially if you make a substantial income from it. You may think you are okay, but you are very wrong. If you are caught, you will have to pay, but you could also pay extra for taxes and interest that bypass the assets in your possession. I am not an accountant-taxman I know of real estate laws in your state, but I know what you need to discuss with your accountant and also some steps you can take if you make your own taxes.

The main problem with making taxes for yourself is that you do not know the tax laws. You might think you made $ 5,000, but that's just gross income before taxes. Many companies have problems with paying taxes because it destroys the bottom line, but they need to be paid. There are two basic classifications that you can enter the house by throwing in; the first of which are independent taxes and short-term capital gains. You prefer to be included in the short-term capital Game section because you pay less taxes. If you are self-employed, you need to start paying as much tax as a business.

To understand how you feel, you need to look at some elements. First, you need to see how long the Earth is preserved. In addition, you need to keep track of the number of transactions made. Because they will all be real estate transactions, you will probably be in the self-employment section.

You might think you do not have to worry about taxes because you haven't been audited and never will be, but with all the ads on TV, the IRS will start watching Real Estate people to increase revenue.

Some of the people returning homes can earn anywhere from $ 50,000 - $ 150,000 from a single transaction. I predict that the IRS will begin to monitor this market more closely by predicting that ordinary people do not know the tax laws.

Tempted By Low Mortgage Rates? Why Not To Stop Flipping Houses

Mortgage interest continues to fall. Now, at almost 60, it can be extremely tempting to think about changing your investment strategy to buy and store instead of coming back, but the grass doesn't turn greener.

Second BankRate.com the average rate for 30-year fixed loans is only 4 % , with 15-year fixed loans available at just over 3%. Indeed, some mortgage lenders advertise 30-year fixed loans of only 3.25% and 15-year loans of less than 3%. It's time to move into this penthouse, get the ranch or buy this beach villa you've always dreamed of. This is not a bad time to lock in one or two rentals long-term choice for building wealth either. However, there are a number of reasons why you are better off sticking with flipping homes as your main real estate investment strategy.

After the last years of hurricanes and terrorist threats, owners have to worry about protecting their wallets. You could take advantage of today's low mortgage rates and build a huge portfolio of rental properties, but what if a natural disaster occurs or a terrorist attack occurs? You know that insurance is very unlikely to pay off anywhere near what you invested.

We have already seen what market fluctuations can do for even the most sophisticated investor portfolios. While with the flip of the house, there is easy money to earn, whether the market is up or down.

Also, if there's one lesson we all should have learned from the recent slowdown, it's that overhead and debt can bite you in the worst way. So rates are low, but it still means getting into debt. What if unemployment continues to grow with the development of globalization and outsourcing?

The vacancy may continue to increase. You may have a nice pillow, but when it rains, it pours and being hit with more vacancies all at the same time could cripple your real estate empire faster than you think.

On the other hand the tipping of houses is always possible. You never have to worry about mortgage payments.

You will never have to deal with difficult tenants, called at 2 am to change a light bulb or worry about being sued because someone slipped or was injured in a fire in one of your homes.

Also, with the right system, a turnkey automated system, you'll find that cash flows and spreads are much more important when you get home than renting them out. It is low risk, a short cash cycle and allows you to build wealth much faster.

The Perfect Way to Make Profit in the Current Economic Down Turn

If you are looking for legitimate ways with which you can make a lot of money, then it is time to give the real estate business serious consideration. Flipping houses is a great way with which you can make a lot of money.

Even though we are currently facing the current economic recession, if you have some kind of money that is late, you can easily invest in cheap homes. These later followed a good result.

In corporate real estate there are many ways with which you can make a lot of money. The most recommended best way would be to simply buy a property, renovate the place and sell it for a profit. If you want to avoid overwork, you can simply sell it as it is at a higher price or you can decide to rent it.

While this may seem like a pretty hard job to do, if you know what to do when it comes to repairing and reselling, you're sure to make a decent profit. It is a good idea to take a look at the real estate that is available in your area.

Another approach that you can take will include simply looking online at various real estate sites. It is also a good idea to take a look at some auction sites and find a good deal.

The idea is to renovate the house that you can then sell for a profit. To increase the chances of increasing the profit margin, try to look for a cheap house that has potential, but does not require much work. This means that you will be limiting your spending amounts in terms of spending, which will allow you to maximize your profits.

Your earnings vary depending on how you go about the whole process. The price you get the house for will play a huge role just like the amount of opportunities you can get when it comes to renovating the place.

To earn money in this type of business requires the right experience and time.

Avoiding Dealer Status When Flipping Houses

Any investor touring more than one or two properties a year will face the problem of being marked" state dealer" by the IRS for tax purposes. He's dangerous. Traders, like realtors, are considered self-employed and subject to taxes on self-employment of 15.3%. Worse still, a retailer cannot pay taxes in installments when using proprietary financing. All rights must be paid in advance on the property, even if the payment has not yet been received.

The most important factors that the IRS seems to use to determine if someone is a realtor or less is the frequency of the sale of real estate, the number of properties sold in a year, and whether there is continuity in the process suggest that the properties of the investment is the actual intention of the company. If the properties are held for more than a year before their sale, it may also weigh against considering an investor's business as that of a "retailer."

There are several ways to handle a significant number of transactions per year, while maintaining the tax benefits of being an investor as opposed to a retailer:

1. Return the property through a joint venture, a self-managed IRA, a Coverdell Education Savings Account, or a 401k-only plan. In a public limited company, only the general manager will be considered a reseller. Trusts and various types of self-managed pension and savings accounts are considered passive investments, and such schemes do not take an active participation in an enterprise.

2. Form a joint venture agreement with an investor or active agent that essentially creates a "Made for You" investment strategy for buying and wholesaling. This joint venture partner may be considered a "reseller", but if you or your entity are not in action, you will not be directly involved in a proprietary flipping business.

3. Put each property in a separate LLC or trust and transfer the LLC or trust rather than the property that is in the entity.

4. At the very least, be sure to separate your wholesale repair and rolling business from other commercial activities such as purchase and maintenance operations or any offer that will result in a sale.

Planning how to finance and own your property can be essential to determine the success of your real estate investment as the actual selection of the property you decide to buy. Being marked with dealer status could cost a lot of time in the long run. Be sure to bid smartly!

There are tons of ways to make money in real estate, but all are useless unless you have a steady stream of motivated sellers and skilled buyers entering your business. When you have a solid pipeline of prospects, choose the best of the best and eventually take control of your financial future. Discover the most effective ways to get your roaring real estate investment business and turn it into an absolute cash engine.

Flipping Homes With Wholesale Loans

Flip house investors often need to take out a loan to buy the property they are launching.

Some investors have enough money to pay cash for a property or use a line of credit, but may take several years before an investor is able to set up this type of financial support. You will need to make use of a loan or mortgage. Wholesale loans are some of the best ways to get home.

In exchange for the opportunity to get a quick loan, in a few days, hard money lenders will charge a higher interest rate on this loan and a high original fee.

However, many flippers trying to make money flipping homes prefer hard money loans because they often finance up to 100% of the purchase price of the property.

HML are often private investors or companies that lend money to people based on ownership or business that money will be safe.

This is a much faster way to get money for a real estate investment than going through the red strip in the bank. In addition, lenders usually look at the type of transaction you have or the potential resale value of the property when granting a loan instead of your credit score.

How long does it take to get the money?

You can access a wholesale loan within 3 days of receiving the final documentation for a loan application.

This allows investors to move quickly on a real estate transaction they find.

How Much Money Can I Get?

Hmls usually only give wholesale loans up to 70% of the value after repair (ARV) of a property.

This is about 30% less than the sale price of the property once you get rehabbed and placed on the real estate market.

This practice helps to ensure that an investor will be able to repay the loan and still make money by launching homes.

What is the average interest rate on a large loan?

Wholesale loans can charge anywhere from 12% to 18% interest on the loan amount.

For a loan with 18% interest that can be a 5% original fee, plus 12% per annum.

How long do I have to repay the loan?

Wholesale loans may vary in duration.

When you take a loan with the HML, you usually write a note for anywhere between 3 and 12 months.

It really depends on the lender and how long you need to make money flipping homes with these loans.

Will I have to face other costs?

Yes, most HML will require there to be a title policy, property insurance and property valuation.

You will also need to put some money on the loan.

So you should wait to pay the original points, discount points and other closing costs before you get the loan. You know what they say, it takes money to make money by flipping through houses!

Will I make regular payments on the loan?

Most of these loans will only be for 3 months to a year.

During this period, you will make interest payments on the loan.

That is, just to pay interest on the loan. At the time you sell the property, you will repay HML the entire loan amount plus the remaining interest on the loan.

You may be able to postpone the interest at the end of the loan, if you have completed the activity with them.

Do I have to worry about credit?

HML checks your credit, but they don't look at your credit score. Instead, they look at your history for proof of failure, seizures, off charge and collection agency lists. They just want to know if you have a history of jumping on repayment loans and bad loans.

It is possible to have a low credit score, but do not have negative scores on your credit history. Thus, wholesale loans are a good option for young real estate investors and those who usually do not bring a lot of credit.

Wholesale loans are a great way for investors to collect home property flip on fast. It is not a good idea for an investor to keep them in the long term because of the high interest rate. If, it is a good practice for those who own the property to return it.

Kind reader,

Thank you very much. I hope you enjoyed the book.

Can I ask you a big favor?

I would be grateful if you would please take a few minutes to leave me a gold star on Amazon.

Thank you again for your support.

Harrison Moore

www.ingramcontent.com/pod-product-compliance
Lightning Source LLC
Chambersburg PA
CBHW08045822O526
45465CB00006B/2306